In Loving Memory of:

_____

I'll always remember...

I'll always remember...

I'll always remember...

I'll always remember...

DATE:

Today I feel:　　○ Sad　○ Tired　○ Teary　○ Angry　○ Neutral　○ Anxious

My energy is:　　○ High　○ So-So　○ Low　○ What energy?

What I remembered about you today...

I wish I could tell you or ask you...

Today was difficult because...

Thoughts…

DATE:

Today I feel: ○ Sad ○ Tired ○ Teary ○ Angry ○ Neutral ○ Anxious

My energy is: ○ High ○ So-So ○ Low ○ What energy?

What I remembered about you today...

I wish I could tell you or ask you...

Today was difficult because...

Thoughts...

DATE:

Today I feel: ○ Sad ○ Tired ○ Teary ○ Angry ○ Neutral ○ Anxious

My energy is: ○ High ○ So-So ○ Low ○ What energy?

What I remembered about you today...

I wish I could tell you or ask you...

Today was difficult because...

Thoughts...

DATE:

Today I feel: ○ Sad   ○ Tired   ○ Teary   ○ Angry   ○ Neutral   ○ Anxious

My energy is: ○ High   ○ So-So   ○ Low   ○ What energy?

What I remembered about you today...

I wish I could tell you or ask you...

Today was difficult because...

Thoughts...

DATE:

Today I feel: ○ Sad   ○ Tired   ○ Teary   ○ Angry   ○ Neutral   ○ Anxious

My energy is: ○ High   ○ So-So   ○ Low   ○ What energy?

What I remembered about you today...

I wish I could tell you or ask you...

Today was difficult because...

Thoughts...

DATE:

Today I feel: ○ Sad ○ Tired ○ Teary ○ Angry ○ Neutral ○ Anxious

My energy is: ○ High ○ So-So ○ Low ○ What energy?

What I remembered about you today...

I wish I could tell you or ask you...

Today was difficult because...

Thoughts...

DATE:

Today I feel: ○ Sad ○ Tired ○ Teary ○ Angry ○ Neutral ○ Anxious

My energy is: ○ High ○ So-So ○ Low ○ What energy?

What I remembered about you today...

I wish I could tell you or ask you...

Today was difficult because...

Thoughts...

DATE:

Today I feel: ○ Sad   ○ Tired   ○ Teary   ○ Angry   ○ Neutral   ○ Anxious

My energy is: ○ High   ○ So-So   ○ Low   ○ What energy?

What I remembered about you today...

I wish I could tell you or ask you...

Today was difficult because...

Thoughts...

DATE:

Today I feel: ○ Sad ○ Tired ○ Teary ○ Angry ○ Neutral ○ Anxious

My energy is: ○ High ○ So-So ○ Low ○ What energy?

What I remembered about you today...

I wish I could tell you or ask you...

Today was difficult because...

Thoughts...

DATE:

Today I feel: ○ Sad ○ Tired ○ Teary ○ Angry ○ Neutral ○ Anxious

My energy is: ○ High ○ So-So ○ Low ○ What energy?

What I remembered about you today...

I wish I could tell you or ask you...

Today was difficult because...

Thoughts…

DATE:

Today I feel:　　○ Sad　○ Tired　○ Teary　○ Angry　○ Neutral　○ Anxious

My energy is:　　○ High　○ So-So　○ Low　○ What energy?

What I remembered about you today...

I wish I could tell you or ask you...

Today was difficult because...

Thoughts...

DATE:

Today I feel: ○ Sad ○ Tired ○ Teary ○ Angry ○ Neutral ○ Anxious

My energy is: ○ High ○ So-So ○ Low ○ What energy?

What I remembered about you today...

I wish I could tell you or ask you...

Today was difficult because...

Thoughts…

DATE:

Today I feel: ○ Sad   ○ Tired   ○ Teary   ○ Angry   ○ Neutral   ○ Anxious
My energy is: ○ High   ○ So-So   ○ Low   ○ What energy?

What I remembered about you today...

I wish I could tell you or ask you...

Today was difficult because...

Thoughts...

DATE:

Today I feel:　　○ Sad　○ Tired　○ Teary　○ Angry　○ Neutral　○ Anxious

My energy is:　　○ High　○ So-So　○ Low　○ What energy?

What I remembered about you today...

I wish I could tell you or ask you...

Today was difficult because...

Thoughts...

DATE:

Today I feel: ○ Sad ○ Tired ○ Teary ○ Angry ○ Neutral ○ Anxious
My energy is: ○ High ○ So-So ○ Low ○ What energy?

What I remembered about you today...

I wish I could tell you or ask you...

Today was difficult because...

Thoughts…

DATE:

Today I feel: ○ Sad   ○ Tired   ○ Teary   ○ Angry   ○ Neutral   ○ Anxious
My energy is: ○ High   ○ So-So   ○ Low   ○ What energy?

What I remembered about you today...

I wish I could tell you or ask you...

Today was difficult because...

Thoughts...

DATE:

Today I feel: ○ Sad   ○ Tired   ○ Teary   ○ Angry   ○ Neutral   ○ Anxious

My energy is: ○ High   ○ So-So   ○ Low   ○ What energy?

What I remembered about you today...

I wish I could tell you or ask you...

Today was difficult because...

Thoughts...

DATE:

Today I feel: ○ Sad   ○ Tired   ○ Teary   ○ Angry   ○ Neutral   ○ Anxious

My energy is: ○ High   ○ So-So   ○ Low   ○ What energy?

What I remembered about you today...

I wish I could tell you or ask you...

Today was difficult because...

Thoughts...

DATE:

Today I feel: ○ Sad   ○ Tired   ○ Teary   ○ Angry   ○ Neutral   ○ Anxious

My energy is: ○ High   ○ So-So   ○ Low   ○ What energy?

What I remembered about you today...

I wish I could tell you or ask you...

Today was difficult because...

Thoughts…

DATE:

Today I feel: ○ Sad   ○ Tired   ○ Teary   ○ Angry   ○ Neutral   ○ Anxious

My energy is: ○ High   ○ So-So   ○ Low   ○ What energy?

What I remembered about you today...

_____

_____

_____

_____

_____

I wish I could tell you or ask you...

_____

_____

_____

_____

_____

Today was difficult because...

_____

_____

_____

_____

_____

Thoughts...

DATE:

Today I feel: ○ Sad   ○ Tired   ○ Teary   ○ Angry   ○ Neutral   ○ Anxious
My energy is: ○ High   ○ So-So   ○ Low   ○ What energy?

What I remembered about you today...

I wish I could tell you or ask you...

Today was difficult because...

Thoughts…

DATE:

Today I feel: ○ Sad   ○ Tired   ○ Teary   ○ Angry   ○ Neutral   ○ Anxious
My energy is: ○ High   ○ So-So   ○ Low   ○ What energy?

What I remembered about you today...

I wish I could tell you or ask you...

Today was difficult because...

Thoughts...

DATE:

Today I feel: ○ Sad ○ Tired ○ Teary ○ Angry ○ Neutral ○ Anxious
My energy is: ○ High ○ So-So ○ Low ○ What energy?

What I remembered about you today...

I wish I could tell you or ask you...

Today was difficult because...

Thoughts...

DATE:

Today I feel: ○ Sad   ○ Tired   ○ Teary   ○ Angry   ○ Neutral   ○ Anxious
My energy is: ○ High   ○ So-So   ○ Low   ○ What energy?

What I remembered about you today...

I wish I could tell you or ask you...

Today was difficult because...

Thoughts...

DATE:

Today I feel: ○ Sad   ○ Tired   ○ Teary   ○ Angry   ○ Neutral   ○ Anxious

My energy is: ○ High   ○ So-So   ○ Low   ○ What energy?

What I remembered about you today...

I wish I could tell you or ask you...

Today was difficult because...

Thoughts...

DATE:

Today I feel: ○ Sad ○ Tired ○ Teary ○ Angry ○ Neutral ○ Anxious

My energy is: ○ High ○ So-So ○ Low ○ What energy?

What I remembered about you today...

I wish I could tell you or ask you...

Today was difficult because...

Thoughts…

DATE:

Today I feel: ○ Sad   ○ Tired   ○ Teary   ○ Angry   ○ Neutral   ○ Anxious
My energy is: ○ High   ○ So-So   ○ Low   ○ What energy?

What I remembered about you today...

I wish I could tell you or ask you...

Today was difficult because...

Thoughts...

DATE:

Today I feel: ○ Sad   ○ Tired   ○ Teary   ○ Angry   ○ Neutral   ○ Anxious
My energy is: ○ High   ○ So-So   ○ Low   ○ What energy?

What I remembered about you today...

I wish I could tell you or ask you...

Today was difficult because...

Thoughts…

DATE:

Today I feel: ○ Sad ○ Tired ○ Teary ○ Angry ○ Neutral ○ Anxious

My energy is: ○ High ○ So-So ○ Low ○ What energy?

What I remembered about you today...

I wish I could tell you or ask you...

Today was difficult because...

Thoughts...

DATE:

Today I feel: ○ Sad ○ Tired ○ Teary ○ Angry ○ Neutral ○ Anxious

My energy is: ○ High ○ So-So ○ Low ○ What energy?

What I remembered about you today...

I wish I could tell you or ask you...

Today was difficult because...

Thoughts…

DATE:

Today I feel: ○ Sad   ○ Tired   ○ Teary   ○ Angry   ○ Neutral   ○ Anxious
My energy is: ○ High   ○ So-So   ○ Low   ○ What energy?

What I remembered about you today...

I wish I could tell you or ask you...

Today was difficult because...

Thoughts...

DATE:

Today I feel: ○ Sad   ○ Tired   ○ Teary   ○ Angry   ○ Neutral   ○ Anxious

My energy is: ○ High   ○ So-So   ○ Low   ○ What energy?

What I remembered about you today...

I wish I could tell you or ask you...

Today was difficult because...

Thoughts...

DATE:

Today I feel:　　○ Sad　○ Tired　○ Teary　○ Angry　○ Neutral　○ Anxious

My energy is:　　○ High　○ So-So　○ Low　○ What energy?

What I remembered about you today...

I wish I could tell you or ask you...

Today was difficult because...

Thoughts…

DATE:

Today I feel: ○ Sad   ○ Tired   ○ Teary   ○ Angry   ○ Neutral   ○ Anxious

My energy is: ○ High   ○ So-So   ○ Low   ○ What energy?

What I remembered about you today...

I wish I could tell you or ask you...

Today was difficult because...

Thoughts...

DATE:

Today I feel: ○ Sad ○ Tired ○ Teary ○ Angry ○ Neutral ○ Anxious

My energy is: ○ High ○ So-So ○ Low ○ What energy?

What I remembered about you today...

_____

_____

_____

_____

_____

I wish I could tell you or ask you...

_____

_____

_____

_____

_____

Today was difficult because...

_____

_____

_____

_____

_____

Thoughts...

DATE:

Today I feel: ○ Sad   ○ Tired   ○ Teary   ○ Angry   ○ Neutral   ○ Anxious

My energy is: ○ High   ○ So-So   ○ Low   ○ What energy?

What I remembered about you today...

I wish I could tell you or ask you...

Today was difficult because...

Thoughts...

DATE:

Today I feel: ○ Sad   ○ Tired   ○ Teary   ○ Angry   ○ Neutral   ○ Anxious

My energy is: ○ High   ○ So-So   ○ Low   ○ What energy?

What I remembered about you today...

I wish I could tell you or ask you...

Today was difficult because...

Thoughts…

DATE:

Today I feel: ○ Sad   ○ Tired   ○ Teary   ○ Angry   ○ Neutral   ○ Anxious
My energy is: ○ High   ○ So-So   ○ Low   ○ What energy?

What I remembered about you today...

I wish I could tell you or ask you...

Today was difficult because...

Thoughts...

DATE:

Today I feel: ○ Sad   ○ Tired   ○ Teary   ○ Angry   ○ Neutral   ○ Anxious

My energy is: ○ High   ○ So-So   ○ Low   ○ What energy?

What I remembered about you today...

I wish I could tell you or ask you...

Today was difficult because...

Thoughts...

DATE:

Today I feel: ○ Sad   ○ Tired   ○ Teary   ○ Angry   ○ Neutral   ○ Anxious
My energy is: ○ High   ○ So-So   ○ Low   ○ What energy?

What I remembered about you today...

I wish I could tell you or ask you...

Today was difficult because...

Thoughts...

DATE:

Today I feel: ○ Sad ○ Tired ○ Teary ○ Angry ○ Neutral ○ Anxious

My energy is: ○ High ○ So-So ○ Low ○ What energy?

What I remembered about you today...

I wish I could tell you or ask you...

Today was difficult because...

Thoughts...

DATE:

Today I feel: ○ Sad ○ Tired ○ Teary ○ Angry ○ Neutral ○ Anxious

My energy is: ○ High ○ So-So ○ Low ○ What energy?

What I remembered about you today...

I wish I could tell you or ask you...

Today was difficult because...

Thoughts...

DATE:

Today I feel: ○ Sad   ○ Tired   ○ Teary   ○ Angry   ○ Neutral   ○ Anxious

My energy is: ○ High   ○ So-So   ○ Low   ○ What energy?

What I remembered about you today...

I wish I could tell you or ask you...

Today was difficult because...

Thoughts...

DATE:

Today I feel: ○ Sad ○ Tired ○ Teary ○ Angry ○ Neutral ○ Anxious

My energy is: ○ High ○ So-So ○ Low ○ What energy?

What I remembered about you today...

I wish I could tell you or ask you...

Today was difficult because...

Thoughts...

DATE:

Today I feel: ○ Sad ○ Tired ○ Teary ○ Angry ○ Neutral ○ Anxious

My energy is: ○ High ○ So-So ○ Low ○ What energy?

What I remembered about you today...

I wish I could tell you or ask you...

Today was difficult because...

Thoughts...

DATE:

Today I feel: ○ Sad ○ Tired ○ Teary ○ Angry ○ Neutral ○ Anxious

My energy is: ○ High ○ So-So ○ Low ○ What energy?

What I remembered about you today...

I wish I could tell you or ask you...

Today was difficult because...

Thoughts...

DATE:

Today I feel:　　○ Sad　○ Tired　○ Teary　○ Angry　○ Neutral　○ Anxious

My energy is:　　○ High　○ So-So　○ Low　○ What energy?

What I remembered about you today...

I wish I could tell you or ask you...

Today was difficult because...

Thoughts...

DATE:

Today I feel: ○ Sad ○ Tired ○ Teary ○ Angry ○ Neutral ○ Anxious

My energy is: ○ High ○ So-So ○ Low ○ What energy?

What I remembered about you today...

I wish I could tell you or ask you...

Today was difficult because...

Thoughts...

DATE:

Today I feel: ○ Sad   ○ Tired   ○ Teary   ○ Angry   ○ Neutral   ○ Anxious

My energy is: ○ High   ○ So-So   ○ Low   ○ What energy?

What I remembered about you today...

I wish I could tell you or ask you...

Today was difficult because...

Thoughts...

DATE:

Today I feel: ○ Sad   ○ Tired   ○ Teary   ○ Angry   ○ Neutral   ○ Anxious
My energy is: ○ High   ○ So-So   ○ Low   ○ What energy?

What I remembered about you today...

I wish I could tell you or ask you...

Today was difficult because...

Thoughts…

Artwork by Vecteezy.com